M000084179

Christmas Is Coming

A Devotional Journey Through Advent

Christopher Greer

Christmas Is Coming is dedicated to Will, Sandy, Lea, Steve, Elle, Sean, Kasey, Afam, Floyd, Grace, Keenan, Jen, Danny, George, and the people of St. Andrew's Presbyterian Church in Newport Beach, California.

Your support, wisdom, and friendship have made it possible for me to study, lead, and write.

The incarnation was first realized in Christ 2000 years ago, but it continues today in you.

Christmas Is Coming

Preface

Before you begin reading, a short introduction about the kind of book this is and how to best use it will be helpful.

Christmas Is Coming is a devotional book organized around daily Scripture readings having to do with the events, prophecy, and meaning of Jesus Christ's birth.

Christmas Is Coming is designed to begin on December 1 and conclude with a reading and reflection on Christmas Day.

Each day begins with a Scripture passage. Start by carefully and prayerfully reading the day's Bible passage; then read the devotion that accompanies it. Only the Scripture references are given—the passages themselves are not printed in this book. That way you can locate, highlight, and make notes around each passage in your own Bible. *To be familiar with God, we must be familiar with Scripture, and reading directly from the Bible helps us in that pursuit.*

Each day concludes with questions and instructions for reflection. Use this section thoughtfully, and it will help you focus on what God says in that day's passage and how he wants to lead you and change you by it.

The words in this book are written to help illuminate and point to Scripture. When they accomplish this task, make use of what you've read. When they do not, set them aside and focus on what God teaches you in the Scripture passage alone. The Holy Spirit is the best guide!

Don't read alone. God has not designed you to be alone during this or any other time of year. Use *Christmas Is Coming* to guide your friends, family, colleagues, Bible study group, or entire church through Advent. Gather regularly with others to talk about what God is teaching each of you and what each person is experiencing as you prepare to celebrate Christmas.

I began praying for each reader the moment I typed these words. My prayer then was the same as it is now: I am asking God to use his Scripture and this copy of *Christmas Is Coming* to reveal himself to you this winter, just as he revealed himself to the world two thousand years ago. I hope that over the next twenty-five days, you will reflect on God's grace anew, allow it to change your life, and share it with everyone you can.

Christopher Greer

Introduction

No person or event in all human history has changed the world as dramatically and finally as Jesus Christ. Many disagree about who he was, why he came, and whether or not he was God, but none can deny that the first-century Jew named Jesus transformed the world. And for those who know him personally, none will deny that he has transformed their lives. These transformations in history and in people found their beginning two thousand years ago when Jesus burst into his creation as a helpless baby.

Christians have recognized and celebrated Advent for a long, long time. The word *advent* literally means "coming," or "arrival," but for Christians it is also the name given to the four weeks that precede Christmas Day. Each year Christ followers around the world fill these four weeks with attentive anticipation and spiritual preparation for Christmas, the celebration of Jesus' arrival.

Christmas Is Coming will help you reflect on the meaning and mystery of the Savior's birth. Whether this is your first time intentionally walking through Advent or your one hundredth, this devotional guide through Scripture will help you peek into the manger at the child who changed everything.

December 1

Isaiah 9:1–7

The One We Wait For

Kids understand Advent well. They may not grasp all the spiritual implications, but they appreciate well the angst of looking forward to something so joyful that the waiting is almost painful. For American children, Christmas is as much about the waiting as it is the day. Christmas morning never seems to come, and as soon as it does, it's gone, and the waiting begins again. The average eight-year-old does not think of New Year's Eve as the night before New Year's Day—it's just the 358th night before next year's Christmas Day! Christmas can never come soon enough.

Our ancient predecessors, the people of Israel, understood this kind of waiting. Like our children during the Yuletide, they ached for the day the Messiah would come. He had been repeatedly promised, and they lived in hopeful expectancy of the day, month, year, decade, and century in which he would finally arrive. Today's beautiful passage from the prophet Isaiah gives us a glimpse into the kind of world that Messiah would usher in:

> He would bring an end to darkness and despair (9:1).

> He would heal the blind and bring hope in the face of death (9:2).

He would be the hope of his people, and he would increase their number to well beyond that of the nation of Israel alone (9:3).

He would bring relief and rest from oppression and burden (9:4).

And he would bring the possibility of peace (9:5).

But as is often the case with God, that which he brings comes differently than we imagine it will. In Isaiah's time he had built a nation from a childless old man (see Genesis 12:1–3), he had defied Pharaoh and delivered his people through a poor-spoken desert dweller (see Exodus 3–15), he had chosen the last and least of Jesse's sons to reign as king (see 1 Samuel 16:1–13), and he had spoken to his people through a variety of men and women who, apart from God's calling and anointing, were a bunch of misfits.

Yet the greatest mystery of all is how his greatest accomplishment of all came to us in the weakest form of all: "A child is born to us" (9:6).

A child. Not an angel. Not a king or a queen. Not a general or a politician or a wealthy and powerful individual wielding great respect and authority.

Sure, Isaiah said, "The government will rest on his shoulders. And he will be called: Wonderful Counselor, Mighty God, Everlasting Father, Prince of Peace. His government and its peace will never end. He will rule with fairness and justice from the throne of his ancestor David for all eternity" (9:6–7). That's true. Messiah was, and is, all these things.

But first he was a child. And the child Israel waited to celebrate then is the child we anticipate and celebrate again this Advent. The Wonderful Counselor, Mighty God, Everlasting Father, and Prince of Peace that the people of God longed for has come to us in the most mysterious yet familiar of packages, and if we listen closely as we read and reflect over the next twenty-five days together, we will begin to hear "Father, forgive them" (Luke 23:34) and "It is finished!" (John 19:30) resonating in his cries from the manger.

REFLECTION

Has God ever brought you something you were waiting for in an unexpected way?

Spend some time in prayer. First, thank God for sending Jesus to put an end to darkness. Second, ask him to help you keep your heart and mind open to the unexpected ways he will provide for your needs this Advent season.

8

December 2

Micah 5:2–5; Isaiah 7:13–16; Isaiah 53

The Unexpected

Among the Old Testament prophecies about Jesus we find a disturbing pattern:

> But you, O Bethlehem Ephrathah, are only a small village among all the people of Judah. (Micah 5:2)

> Look! The virgin will conceive a child! (Isaiah 7:14)

> There was nothing beautiful or majestic about his appearance, nothing to attract us to him. (Isaiah 53:2)

Do you see what I mean by "disturbing pattern?" Let me try to be clearer.

The book you are reading is titled *Christmas Is Coming* because it was written to help us celebrate the birth of Jesus—the Creator, Savior, and King of humankind. The whole Bible points to this Jesus, and we Christians believe that he is God. We stake our lives on the fact that he was (and still is) powerful enough, courageous enough, and righteous enough to defeat death forever. For us, Jesus is sort of a big deal.

If you were an Old Testament prophet charged with helping prepare the world for the arrival of this magnificent Jesus, God himself in the flesh, would you have announced (much less actually written down) that he would be born in a backwater country town that no one in the first century ever bragged about? Would you have been bold enough to predict that he would be born to a virgin?

If you wanted to convince your listeners that he was going to be the most important person ever, would you have described him as a less-than-handsome, not-so-special average Joe? Me neither. Yet long before he arrived, the Old Testament described the one hope for humankind as a run-of-the-mill fella from an insignificant town, born to an anything-but-royal kind of family.

Think about how the birth announcement of an eminent person would go today. We live in a world in which we expect our leaders and culture influencers to have strong pedigrees. We expect them to have the best education, work the best jobs, live in the best places, and have the best looks. We even expect this of ourselves! We are self-conscious if we are from uninteresting places, lack dynamic families, attended non-prestigious schools, or have low-paying professions. We are even a bit embarrassed about our church if it is not a young, growing, and "relevant" mega-church.

But if there is one thing we will learn about Jesus in Advent, it is that he defies the expected and embodies the unexpected. The Messiah did not come from a place we expected, in the way we expected, or to the people we expected. And he certainly did not do what we expected.

God used the unexpected to grab our attention, and when he got it, he recalibrated our expectations so that we would not miss out on what he was doing. He does the same today. If we look around, we will see this unpredictable God in unexpected places. His joy often abounds in suffering, his presence is found in loneliness, his peace moves in uncertainty, and his family develops from the most unlikely fellow travelers.

When Jesus arrived, he was a typical child in an insignificant town, well outside the royal family. Yet he is the most significant person ever to live. He changed the world, and in his unexpected way he is still changing lives today.

REFLECTION

In what unexpected ways has God shown up in your life? Has Jesus ever transformed something that seemed insignificant in your life into something significant?

Spend a few moments thanking God for the way he defies the expected. Maybe praying the following prayer will help:

King of the universe,

Thank you for coming to us in ways we never expected and for exceeding our expectations again and again. I admit that I often imagine that you are smaller and more insignificant than you really are. Forgive me for thinking less of you than I should. Help me to see you in the small and big things in life and to expect significant things in insignificant places. You are a God of surprises. Thank you for the life-changing surprise of your love for someone like me—someone who often feels insignificant but whom you make significant because you have created and redeemed me.

I love you, Jesus. Amen.

December 3

Matthew 1:18–24

Change of Plans

Have you ever caught yourself daydreaming? While *driving*? No one in his or her right mind would say that this is a safe practice, but no one would deny having done it. It is easy for us to lose ourselves in a drive we've made again and again. Countless times I have driven to work, to the grocery store, or to my favorite restaurant, and I can clearly remember getting in the car and back out of it, but I can't remember *anything* in between. Yet most would correctly argue that it is the "in between" that is most important: turns, stoplights, cars, not to mention pedestrians!

Somehow I have become so familiar with my routes that when I drive them, my mind goes into auto pilot. I can successfully accomplish the task at hand and still miss all the details along the way. The same thing can happen when we read familiar Bible passages.

If you have been a Christian for a long time, the Bible verses in today's devotion may be very familiar to you. You may know them by memory. Therein lies the need for an important warning: *as you read today's Scripture passage, be sure that you did not successfully accomplish the task at hand yet miss all the details along the way.*

If we are not careful, our familiarity with the story of Christmas will cause us to miss what we need to see. With that in mind, it might be helpful to reread today's passage.

When I slowed down to notice the details of this familiar Christmas passage, I found much to ponder. Here are just a few examples:

> Jesus, God in the flesh, was *born* (1:18). That is an awe-filling wonder in and of itself.
>
> His earthly mother was a real human woman (1:18).
>
> And she was a virgin (1:18)!
>
> Joseph had a conversation. With an *angel* (1:20).
>
> In that conversation Joseph learned that the boy he would be given to raise would save the world from sin (1:21). Wow!
>
> A prophet of God had predicted some of these details *seven hundred* years before they happened (1:22–23).

These are just a few important and faith-building details, and each is worthy of greater reflection. But as I read these verses, there was one detail that stood out to me for the first time. In the second half of verse 20, the angel of the Lord told Joseph, "Do not be afraid to take Mary as your wife. For the child within her was conceived by the Holy Spirit."

Let me pose a question: have you ever mapped out a journey for your future—set goals and laid out an exciting and fulfilling path for the years ahead—and then had those plans erased or completely changed in the blink of an eye by God?

I have. And I must confess that change stresses me out, even when it is initiated by God. So it is difficult for me to imagine all that must have been running through Joseph's mind when Mary revealed her pregnancy to him. Obviously this had not been part of his plan! Joseph's anxiety was amplified one hundredfold because he and Mary lived in the first century, when sex out of wedlock was a shameful disgrace for the entire family and women were stoned to death for adultery.

Before the smoke from Joseph's incinerated dreams had even begun to clear, he was visited by an angel of God. But instead of hearing empathetic words that soothed his pain and affirmed his desire to quietly annul his engagement to Mary, the angel told him, "Do not be afraid to take Mary as your wife" (1:20). Mary's future-altering and gossip-igniting pregnancy was the work of God himself, and so the Lord encouraged Joseph to face the challenge and accept his rewritten future as a participant in the humanity-saving work of God.

Joseph's response convicts me: "When Joseph woke up, he did as the angel of the Lord commanded and took Mary as his wife" (1:24).

Joseph recognized the voice of the Lord and trusted God. Despite his fear and uncertainty, he let go of his expectations and became the earthly guardian of Jesus the Messiah.

Oh, that we would lay aside our plans and walk into the future God writes for us! What great joy awaits us.

I wonder now, as I reflect on Joseph's self-sacrificing obedience to God: when have I been so wrapped up in my own life that I missed playing a role in the life of the one who "will save his people from their sins?" (1:21)

REFLECTION

When has God interrupted your plans for the future? How have you responded to the disruption?

Read James 4:13–16 and spend some time thinking about how James's words and Joseph's actions are similar.

Try something difficult but important. Write down three words or brief phrases that represent three different dreams or plans you have for your future (regarding your spouse, family, profession, retirement, health, or something else). After writing these down, slowly mark a dark line through each one and ask yourself this question: "If God changed any or all of my plans, how would I respond?" Would you trust him and obey? Would you give up on God and pursue your dreams anyway? Spend a few minutes prayerfully reflecting on your honest answers.

December 4

Luke 1:5–17

To Those Who Wait

Zechariah and Elizabeth's story reminds me of the phrase "Good things come to those who wait." Like a number of other popular phrases (for instance, "God helps those who help themselves" or "To thine own self be true"), this one is commonly mistaken as a biblical teaching. But with a little etymological research, one quickly learns that it's a knockoff.

The confusion surrounding the not-so-biblical roots of "Good things come to those who wait" seems to lie in Lamentations 3:25. The English Standard Version translates the verse this way: "The LORD is good to those who wait for him, to the soul who seeks him." Do you see the similarity between the phrase and verse? Do you detect the difference?

Eugene Peterson's translation in *The Message* helps clarify the matter: "*God proves to be good* to the man who *passionately waits*, to the woman who *diligently seeks*."

The Bible makes a crucial correction to this cultural phrase. The difference between Lamentations 3:25 and "Good things come to those who wait" is twofold: first, it is *God* who defines and provides what are good things. Second, the recipient of those good things is to be engaged in a specific kind of waiting. The goodness is not ambiguous, and the waiting is not aimless. God gives what he knows is good, and he gives it to those who wait patiently, passionately, and prayerfully.

Take Zechariah as exhibit A. Luke 1 tells us that Zechariah and his wife Elizabeth had waited a long time for a child. The Scripture says that these two were godly, obedient, and prayerful people, but that "Elizabeth was unable to conceive, and they were both very old" (1:7). Yet God decided it was good for them—who had been passionately waiting, diligently seeking, and quietly hoping—to have a son.

Zechariah and Elizabeth's experience helps teach us what the Lamentations writer knew about waiting on God: "It is good to wait quietly for salvation from the LORD . . . for there may be hope at last" (Lamentations 3:26, 29).

Zechariah's answered prayer—the promise of a son—brought hope not only to him and his wife but also brings hope to all the world. Their son's role, according to the angel who announced the news to Zechariah, would be to "prepare the people for the coming of the Lord" (1:17). The "Lord" the angel was referring to would be none other than Jesus, the one by which lives would be made whole, sin would be defeated, and the world would be redeemed.

Contrary to the phrase with which this entry started, undefined good does not come to those who simply wait long enough. Zechariah and the writer of Lamentations show us that God's good comes to those who patiently and prayerfully wait with expectant hope in him. And Jesus' coming is proof that God's goodness is exceedingly good. His goodness is worth waiting for.

At this moment you may be waiting on something far more significant than just a Christmas holiday. You may be waiting for a cure, for peace, for sobriety, for joy, for friendship, or for God's voice. Today God wants to tell you to keep waiting—but don't *only* wait. He wants you to wait prayerfully, patiently, and passionately. There is hope, and in the end, he is always worth waiting for.

REFLECTION

In *The Message* Eugene Peterson beautifully and faithfully translates Lamentations 3. For today's time with God, read this passage (3:19–32) slowly and reflectively. As you read and pray, highlight the verses that most encourage, comfort, or challenge you. Let them be God's personal word to you.

> I'll never forget the trouble, the utter lostness,
> the taste of ashes, the poison I've swallowed.
>
> I remember it all—oh, how well I remember—
> the feeling of hitting the bottom.
>
> But there's one other thing I remember,
> and remembering, I keep a grip on hope.
>
> GOD's loyal love couldn't have run out,

his merciful love couldn't have dried up.

They're created new every morning.
How great your faithfulness!

I'm sticking with GOD (I say it over and over).
He's all I've got left.

GOD proves to be good to the man who passionately
waits, to the woman who diligently seeks.

It's a good thing to quietly hope,
quietly hope for help from GOD.

It's a good thing when you're young
to stick it out through the hard times.

When life is heavy and hard to take,
go off by yourself. Enter the silence.

Bow in prayer. Don't ask questions:
Wait for hope to appear.

Don't run from trouble. Take it full-face.
The "worst" is never the worst.

Why? Because the Master won't ever
walk out and fail to return.

If he works severely, he also works tenderly.
His stockpiles of loyal love are immense.

December 5

Luke 1:26–38

The Answer to How

Anytime I think God is telling me to do something, inevitably I utter a one-word question: how?

Love your neighbor.
How?

Be the spiritual leader in your home and work.
How?

Seek the best for your opponents, and love your enemies.
How?

Give your time, your money, and your life away to others.
How, how, how?

I find it very comforting that Mary asked the same question (see 1:34). Granted, she was a frightened teenage girl chosen to raise the Savior of mankind, while I am a grown man who is simply asked to love God and my neighbor. Still, I find great comfort in how similar my and Mary's responses are to God. After receiving a remarkable revelation, Mary, just like I do, asked, "How?"

But for all the comfort I find in asking the same question as Mary, I find much more comfort in God's answer. In verse

35 God answers Mary's question and mine: "The Holy Spirit will come upon you, and the power of the Most High will overshadow you."

God never, ever asks us to do his work for him. When he commands us to do something, or when he injects his will into our fearful lives, he always does so with an accompanying promise. God tells us to do something and then sends us His Spirit with the "power" to "overshadow" us. When we say yes to God, he comes so powerfully that he makes what seems impossible to us possible.

God gave the power to birth and raise the Savior of humankind to a frightened, humble teenager. Similarly, he gives the power to forgive to those who are hurt, angry, and resentful. He gives the power to lead to those who are nervous, insecure, and untrained. He gives the power to pray to those who are selfish, forgetful, and inarticulate. And He gives the power to love to everyone who calls on his name.

The word *overshadow* means "to outshine," or "to render insignificant." As humbling as it may be, our efforts to live a meaningful and useful life are insignificant in light of what God most wants to accomplish through us. Think about this: who was Mary before the angel spoke to her? A teenager engaged to Joseph. Who was she after "the power of the Most High" overshadowed her? The woman who birthed, taught, raised, and nurtured the Messiah. God's power rendered her previous identity insignificant.

Our lives are no different. Before we receive God's power, we are unforgiving, insecure, selfish, and unloving. When his power overshadows us, we become forgiving, selfless, prayerful, and loving. As Paul writes in 2 Corinthians 5:17, "This means that anyone who belongs to Christ has become a new person. The old life is gone; a new life has begun!" All that is required of us is to mirror Mary's humble response to God's will for her: "I am the Lord's servant. May everything you have said about me come true" (1:38).

REFLECTION

Think back to a time when you asked God, "How?" Did you patiently allow him to overshadow you by his Spirit to accomplish his work? Or did you take matters into your own hands? Reflect on what you did and what the results were.

What is God impressing upon you now? Are you allowing him to give you the power to accomplish the how? Why or why not?

December 6

Luke 1:39–45

Celebration

"Does anyone have any prayer requests?"

This sentence often signals the final moments of a small-group Bible study or Sunday school class. It is customary in many Christian traditions to end group meetings with the sharing of prayer requests, and I believe that this is a good thing. After all, Scripture implores, "Confess your sins to each other and pray for each other so that you may be healed" (James 5:16). There is powerful, miracle-working, and saving power in our prayers for one another, particularly when they are coupled with confession.

But I have noticed a distinctive pattern in virtually all the small-group Bible studies in which I have been a member: the moment prayer requests are shared, a dark emotional cloud gathers as if a dreary winter rain has suddenly moved indoors. The group's interaction becomes myopically focused on sickness and pain, unmet expectations, and unfulfilled needs. The members pour out their hearts about all that they wish God would do and all the difficult circumstances that only God can fix.

In my experience we too often focus only on what we want God to do, and we forget to celebrate all the amazing things he is doing or has already done.

25

Why is that? Is it because we think God is a cosmic handyman whom we call only when a problem arises? Is it because when life is easy, we take for granted all that God does to protect and provide for us? Has God become like the ever-present old friend whom we no longer pursue, acknowledge, regard, celebrate, or give meaningful thanks for?

Elizabeth didn't think so. Today's passage reminds me of a birthday cake in too small a box. The sweet and delightful goodness of God's blessing pushes through the cracks— Elizabeth's joy cannot be contained, and she does not hesitate to celebrate what God is doing in Mary's life.

Elizabeth could have responded jealously. Though she was pregnant like Mary, her pregnancy came after decades of waiting while Mary's came before she had finished her teen years. Though Elizabeth's child would be special, it was Mary who carried the Son of God. Yet Elizabeth's response was void of any self-centeredness. She enthusiastically rejoiced for Mary, who was blessed "above all women" (Luke 1:42). Not everyone responds to God's blessing in others' lives as favorably as Elizabeth did.

I know single people who refuse to celebrate the engagement of their friends.

I know jobless people who refuse to celebrate the career moves of their siblings.

I know childless people who refuse to celebrate the new addition to their neighbor's family.

Mary has been chosen by the God of the universe to carry and raise the Messiah, and these are the words Elizabeth has for her: "God has blessed you above all women, and your child is blessed! Why am I so honored, that the mother of my Lord should visit me?" (1:42–43).

Is this how you celebrate when you see God's blessing in the lives of your friends? Or are you too preoccupied with what you do not have to celebrate the good gifts that God is giving to others?

A slight modification to Elizabeth's words renders an important question for all of us to utter this Advent and Christmas season: why are we so honored that the Lord should visit us?!

May we be a people who are overwhelmingly joyful about the coming of our King and about the opportunity for others to feel him moving inside them for the first time.

REFLECTION

One of the reasons we do not adequately celebrate what God is doing in our lives is because we do not stop and intentionally recall it.

Grab a pen and some paper, or turn on your computer, and spend fifteen minutes recording what God is doing and has done in your life. You may want to use the following questions to prompt you:

> What is something God has given that you have not thanked him for recently?
>
> What is something God has done that has joyfully surprised you?
>
> What is something God has done in your life that you know you do not deserve?
>
> What is something God is doing in the life of someone else you know?

Make a note to tell them that you notice it and that you want to thank and praise God for it.

Want to read how Mary responded to God's good news that she held inside her? Read Luke 1:46–55, Mary's song of praise.

Take as much time as you need to thank God for all that he has done in your life (and in others'), and keep your eyes open to the amazing gifts of God as you journey through the rest of this Advent season.

December 7

Luke 2:1–7

Bending Christmas

Can you think of a song, a picture, a story, or even a smell that instantly transports you to another time and place? I have a ton of them. One such trigger is this passage from Luke chapter 2. The moment my eyes see the words, I am taken to the living room of my childhood home on a Christmas morning. The tree is lit, and my brothers and I are sitting on the couch desperately waiting to tear into our gifts. My father's voice, strong and sweet, rings in my ears as he begins our morning by reading the Christmas story. The memory makes me feel warm, happy, and fulfilled.

This is the description of my Christmas experience, and if I'm not careful, my mind will bend the truth of the passage under the weight of my safe, clean, and abundant Christmas experiences. Yet the setting into which Jesus of Nazareth was born is much more like a third-world barrio than a middle-class American home.

Our emotions are powerful, and just as my childhood experience can shape my feelings about this familiar passage, so too can our personal lives and Christmas expectations shape the way we understand the incarnation of Christ. Christmas in America is often about giving and receiving the right gifts, throwing and attending the right parties, even orchestrating and observing the right kinds of worship services.

But Jesus did not come to those who thought they did what was right. He did not come to those who thought they already had it all. Jesus did not come to people who thought they were safe, clean, and living the abundant life. He came to those in need.

The writer of Matthew records a story in which Jesus was grilled by the religious elite for sharing dinner with "disreputable sinners" and "scum." In response, Jesus said, "Healthy people don't need a doctor—sick people do." Then he added, "I have come to call not those who think they are righteous, but those who know they are sinners" (Matthew 9:10–13).

In John 10:10 Jesus famously declares, "My purpose is to give them [us!] a rich and satisfying life." Pair that with Jesus' words in John 14:6—"I am the way, the truth, and the life"—and one begins to understand that Jesus clearly claimed that *he* was the only source for a full and satisfying life.

Jesus came to fill that which is missing in all of us. And therein lies one of the problems of allowing our personal version of Christmas to shape our perspective of the Christ. In this season of lights, food, family, and gifts, we can all too easily forget that Jesus alone is the one who brings true light (John 8:12), gives true food (John 6:35), provides us an eternal family (Ephesians 2:19), and is God's greatest gift (John 3:16).

I'm not suggesting that you abandon family Christmas traditions, delete your secular Christmas music, or forgo any gift buying. Rather, I am encouraging you to celebrate Christ at Christmas with a firm understanding of how he came and why he came, allowing the truth to bend your Christmas experience instead of the other way around.

REFLECTION

Today we have a few tough questions to help us think about how we understand Scripture and Christmas. Find some quiet and uninterrupted time to ponder them:

> What is one cultural experience or influence that shapes the way you understand God or Scripture?

> Why is it difficult for us to keep our own cultural and personal experience separate from how we understand the Bible?

> What is it about the way Jesus came or the reason Jesus came that God is asking you to be more mindful of this Advent season?

Make time today to reread Luke 2:1–7, and use your imagination to picture the town of Bethlehem, the stable or cave where Jesus was born, and the sights and sounds of a poor first-century family giving birth to their first child. Let your imagination carry you to a different, more real experience of Jesus' birth.

What did you notice? What moved you? Why does it matter?

December 8

Luke 2:8–14

The Only Baby That Matters

The tabloids love baby news. Countless words fill the pages of checkout line newspapers each time a movie star, sports figure, or politician becomes a parent to be, and pop-culture magazines explode with "Exclusive Baby Photos!" the moment the newly minted human is carried out of the maximum security hospital. But no newborn has caused a greater international media ruckus than the birth of George Alexander Louis, better known simply as Prince George. The tiny prince's parents are Prince William of Wales, Duke of Cambridge, and Her Royal Highness Catherine, Duchess of Cambridge (Kate Middleton), the famous heirs of the English monarchy.

Prince William and Duchess Kate's every activity, family event, and life announcement is trumpeted around the world to an adoring public who cannot get enough of the good-looking, uber-rich power couple. And the birth of George took the cake.

But the announcement only took the cake for us mortals. The little prince might have captured the attention of a fascinated human public, but there were no heavenly choirs singing birthday songs and no celestial messengers personally inviting commoners to visit him crib-side. Human births matter a great deal to family and friends, but

I can guarantee you this: no baby on the planet (no matter how famous his parents) was heralded the way Jesus was.

Read the following statement very slowly: when Jesus was born, the skies literally opened, and "the armies of heaven" sang "glory to God" (2:13–14). The skies *opened* (what is that even like?!), and real angels sang perfect music *to God* in celebration of it all.

I am not trying to beat a dead Christmas horse here. I am not trying to point out how spectacular the shepherds' experience must have been or convince you that the proclamation of the angels was special. I am trying to do the same thing the angels did. I am trying to point you to Jesus.

You see, when it comes to the birth of a child, none matters as much as Jesus' did. The birth of Prince George doesn't really matter to the world. The birth of the next president of the United States doesn't either. Honestly—and you won't like hearing this—the birth of your own child doesn't matter to the world. It matters a great deal to you (as it should!), and it matters a great deal to God (because he loves every person he creates), but these individuals do not ultimately matter to the world. More rightly put, they don't matter *for* the world.

Angels in heaven announced the birth of Jesus and sang songs of worship to God over it because his birth is the only one that truly matters for the world.

Here's why:

No baby Jesus, no grown-up Jesus.
No birth of Jesus, no death of Jesus.
No incarnated Jesus, no resurrected Jesus.

If there is no Jesus, then there is no hope, no forgiveness, no salvation, no eternal life, no purpose, no freedom, and no love. There may be existence, but there is no meaning.

So when the baby was born who would provide all that, more than just the world and its media paid attention: the very heavens from which he came exploded with the news that the world was changed forever and that there was hope for every man, woman, and child ever born.

Amen.

REFLECTION

Make time today to reflect on these important questions:

Does the birth of Jesus really matter to you? Why or why not?

Do you celebrate his birth as if it matters? How?

Does it matter enough for you to tell other people about him? Who will you tell, and when?

Spend a moment to make this prayer yours:

God of the heavens and of earth,

There is little doubt from your Scripture that Jesus' birth matters more than any other. Help us to understand the gravity of his birth, life, death, and resurrection. If necessary, send your angels again, oh God, so that we might be convinced anew of just how important the celebration of this baby is.

Amen.

December 9

Luke 2:15–20

Ponder with Your Heart

Three days ago we read Luke 1 and experienced Elizabeth's elation and Mary's praise-filled song in response to the news of Mary's pregnancy. In today's Scripture reading we see the shepherds' response to Jesus' birth. These men gave the kind of response that is perfectly apt for the arrival of King Jesus: they ran at breakneck speed to get a closer look at the baby, they told everyone they could about what they had seen, and then they returned to the work that God had given them while "glorifying and praising God for all they had heard and seen" (2:20).

In nine out of ten sermons on this passage, the attention is placed on the shepherds' response. In many ways this is right. After all, wouldn't you agree that the right and good response for anyone who is invited to see a miracle of God would be to take a better look, to enthusiastically share it with others, and then continue with life in constant praise of God for his miracle? What a God-centered reaction. What a powerful witness to the world.

But this time around, that is not the message that captured my attention. For me, the response that stood out most in this passage was Mary's. Look again at verse 19: "Mary kept all these things in her heart and thought about them often."

37

Other translations say that Mary "pondered" these things in her heart. *The Message* says that Mary held "them dear, deep within herself." How often do you ponder the meaningful events of life stored deeply within your heart? How often is your heart like a baker working handmade dough over and over until it is perfectly kneaded?

Lots happens in our hearts. But typically our hearts are the repository of our surface-level reactionary feelings, not the storehouse where we intentionally place our experiences so that we can mull them over and wring out their true meaning.

How often have you merrily enjoyed a birthday party without stopping to think about aging and the meaning of life? When have you attended a wedding without spending significant time pondering what it means to be male and female or what it means to be in covenant relationship?

Honestly, I have way too often spent Easter Sunday reveling in beautiful church music and a delicious brunch without holding the resurrection dear and pondering its meaning deep within myself. I have also opened entirely too many Christmas gifts and attended jovial holiday gatherings without spending more than a moment contemplating and internalizing the birth of Jesus the Christ.

There is room and need for both celebration and reflection. Some of us need to be shepherds and make Christmas a bigger deal this year. We need to celebrate the Christ child, tell our friends all about him, and then return to life in the new year glorifying and praising God for what he has done. Others of us need to make an intentional move toward deeply pondering the things of God. Like Mary, we need to look beyond our celebration and fully mull over the deeper meaning of Christmas.

Which do you need to do this year?

REFLECTION

Prayerfully consider today which people in today's passage you are most like. Are you like the shepherds—is God revealing himself to you in ways that incite you to joyful celebration and storytelling? Or are you like Mary, called by God to consider more deeply all the activities of Christmas?

Write down which of these responses you most identify with, and then either list some specific ways that you will celebrate Christmas more joyfully this year or list the experiences of this Advent and Christmas that you will purposefully reflect on in your heart.

December 10

Luke 2:21–35

Inside and Out

Try to switch places with Mary for a moment. Imagine being told by an angel of God that you would play a major role in God's plan for saving the world—while you were still a teenager. Imagine his plan for you including an out-of-wedlock pregnancy while you lived in a society that stoned women for such things (not to mention that you had not even had sex yet).

Never mind the impossibility of what the angel said—would you have believed that an angel had *actually* appeared to you in the first place? After a vigorous debate with myself about whether to laugh out loud or throw up, I think I would have begun to doubt my own sanity. As soon as my teenage eyes saw an angel, my Texas-accented inner monologue would have said, "It's time for a rest, partner. You've been out in the sun too long."

There is little doubt that Mary experienced deep questions and doubt. And that is part of the reason God sent Simeon to her.

As a Christ follower, I find it a challenge to understand the difference between the Holy Spirit's instruction and my own voice rattling around in my head. I believe that the God of Scripture is the living God, yet I've never felt his physical touch or heard his audible voice. But I am reminded in these passages that prior to his birth, Mary didn't either. So how did Mary know that the angel had truly brought her a message from God and that she was not just going crazy? The same way we do: by experiencing both an internal calling and external confirmation.

Remember Mary's immediate response to the angel's pregnancy announcement? "I am the Lord's servant. May everything you have said about me come true" (Luke 1:38). Before Jesus was born, Mary had been a follower of God and had learned to understand his calling. Thirty years after his birth, Jesus would say, "I know my own sheep, and they know me. . . . My sheep listen to my voice; I know them, and they follow me" (John 10:14, 27). Mary was a fine example of a sheep who knew God's voice, so at the angel's message, she felt an internal calling.

The second way Mary understood God's calling was by external confirmation. Mary received it in several ways:

> Joseph, Mary's fiancé, was also told by an angel that she would bear a son (see Matthew 1:18–25).

> Elizabeth, by the Holy Spirit, confirmed that Mary's unborn child was the Lord (see Luke 1:39–45).

As if that was not enough, confirmation continued to abound after Jesus was delivered:

His birth was announced by a choir of angels (see Luke 2:8–14).

God used a brilliant star to lead distant astrologers to Jesus' manger (see Matthew 2:9–11).

The Holy Spirit gave confirmation of his identity through Simeon and Anna (see Luke 2:25–40).

At twelve years old Jesus' wisdom amazed the religious teachers in the temple (see Luke 2:41–52).

John the Baptist, a prophet of God, saw him and declared, "Look! The Lamb of God who takes away the sin of the world!" (John 1:29).

Even demons recognized and obeyed Jesus' commands, confirming Jesus' identity as God (see Matthew 9:28–34).

The internal message that God gives is an external message that God confirms. The catch is this: external confirmation is only possible when we live open and vulnerable lives in a community of other Jesus followers. To discern God's will we must be faithful listeners, ready to receive God's internal messages, and faithful community members ready to receive and share with others his external confirmation.

REFLECTION

I challenge you this Advent (start today!) to choose someone whom you know well and who is faithful to God, and ask that person to tell you if they see God working in your life and, if so, what he is doing. Don't put the person on the spot; rather, ask him or her to prayerfully think about this and get back to you. When the person does, compare his or her reply to what you feel God is personally calling you to do or be.

I also challenge you to be aware of the community of God around you, to proactively listen to the Spirit of God, and to encourage others in what you see God doing in them. Remember, if you do not act as part of their external confirmation when God prompts you to do so, how will they know if their internal calling is of God?

God is moving in faithful Jesus followers all around you. Are you involved in a community of them?

December 11

Luke 2:36–40

That's Him

Have you ever been asked by a preacher or a fellow church member, "If Jesus walked into this church on a Sunday morning, would we recognize him?"

It is typically a hypothetical question designed to challenge the way we do church on Sundays and test the devotion of individual church members. Sometimes it is asked to prompt true reflection. What would it be like if Jesus appeared, in the flesh, in our midst? And would we actually recognize him?

The problem is that this is a Western, post-Enlightenment question. The Enlightenment taught us to gauge reality by our senses, by physical laws, by what is observable, repeatable, and provable. This question asks us to look for Jesus with our eyes and ears and, ultimately, our intellect. It asks us if we, by our senses, would be able to pick Jesus out of a crowd if he walked onto the scene today.

But this is not how Anna the prophetess recognized Jesus. Anna did not recognize Jesus by her intellect. She recognized Jesus by her heart.

Anna had been in the temple day and night for about fifty years (see 2:36–37). She had seen countless Jewish baby boys brought into the temple for the traditional Jewish ceremony of circumcision, including the eight-day old Jesus (see 2:21). How then did she pick Jesus out of the crowd and know to tell "everyone who had been waiting expectantly" (2:38) that this baby boy was their rescuer?

She did not know it was him because she recognized him physically; she knew it was him because she was ready for him spiritually. Anna "never left the Temple but stayed there day and night, worshiping God with fasting and prayer" (2:37).

Anna remained in the presence of God by her constant worship, fasting, and prayer. And because she lived in God's presence, she was able to recognize his Son when he came into her world.

This is exactly what Advent is all about. It's a time of intentional prayer and patient waiting. It is a time for keeping our eyes open to when and how Jesus will step into our lives. It is a time for continual preparation so that we will be able to recognize the work he is doing in us and in the world around us.

Sometimes the Lord shows up in spectacular ways: the ear-tingling voices of angels in the shepherds' sky, the death-defying touch of Jesus in Lazarus's tomb, or the heart-stopping and life-changing encounter with God on Paul's journey to Damascus. Maybe your first encounter with the Lord was as powerful as these. But more often than not, he comes in a still small voice. And now, as disciples of

Christ, steadily serving the Lord like Anna, Advent is an opportunity for us to worship, fast, pray, and keep our eyes open to see where Jesus, who once quietly came as a tiny child, is present and at work in our lives and in the world today.

A simple truth is found here in Anna's story: knowing the Lord is about constantly spending time in the presence of God. The people I know who easily recognize God when he walks through the doors are those who spend the most time with him *before* he arrives.

REFLECTION

Do you recognize God when he shows up because you have already spent a great amount of time in his presence?

Do you view your relationship with God as an ongoing, evolving, and maturing relationship? Or is it a relationship comprised of random, one-time moments, and highlights?

Do you know how to maintain a constant relationship with God? If not, or if spending time with the Lord is difficult for you, I encourage you to set a time to speak with a pastor, mentor, friend, or family member whose faith you admire and from whom you can learn something about an ongoing, thriving relationship with God through Jesus Christ.

December 12

Matthew 2:1–8, 12

Deeply Disturbed

When you read the words "Jesus in a manger," what images come to your mind?

Let me see if I can guess. You see Mary and Joseph kneeling by their newborn son with a relieved yet awe-filled look on their faces. Your mind's eye pictures weary shepherds and wise men full of worship and delight. An angel floats somewhere near the stable with a knowing expression that says, "See, Mary, I told you that you were going to have a special baby." And at the very center of the picture, wrapped in a cloth and lying in the straw, is the baby Jesus. He is glowing. Literally. He is quiet, content, and smiling.

If asked to describe your manger scene, would you express it as discomforting or even threatening? Would you use the words *troubling* or *deeply disturbing*? Probably not. These are not the emotions typically evoked by the manger scene. Yet those are the words Matthew used to describe King Herod's feelings about Jesus' birth.

The natural question is, why? Why would the king of Israel be troubled and deeply disturbed by the birth of a baby? Wouldn't there have been hundreds of babies born in his kingdom around the same time?

47

Verses 2 and 6 of today's scripture give us the answer. According to the wise men and Herod's priests, little Jesus was far more than a single addition to the kingdom population. He was the newborn "king of the Jews" (2:2), the "ruler" of Israel (2:6).

If you were King Herod—an egocentric megalomaniac who proved that he would do anything and everything to maintain control of his kingdom—the birth of a new "king of the Jews" would be anything but good news. It would be troubling and deeply disturbing news.

Unfortunately, we are not so different from King Herod. Each of us enjoys reigning over our own, private kingdoms, but each and every Christmas we must, like King Herod, face what it means for *Jesus* to be the King. When we do, we are often confronted by our own egocentrism and megalomania.

Most of us are perfectly content with the glow-in-the-dark baby Jesus that we see painted into Renaissance nativity scenes. He radiates innocence, peace, and tranquility. If we are honest with ourselves, those images are no threat to our inner dictators. We have rendered Jesus a benign addition to the "kingdom of [place your name here]." Like Herod, we make ourselves (or our reputation, our job, our family, our bank account, our addiction, our power, or our happiness) the king of our world, and we will do anything and everything to maintain control of our kingdom. As long as Jesus stays in that manger—or stays hanging from a cross—we are content to carry him around as a sentimental token of our Christianity. There he is neither troubling nor deeply disturbing.

But the truth of Christmas is this: Jesus did not stay in that manger. Jesus was God incarnate. He grew into a man, lived a perfect life, and, though he was crucified like a worthless criminal, rose from the grave and defeated sin and death forever. He showed us once and for all that he was not only the King of the Jews but the King of the world, the King over death, the King of your life and mine.

REFLECTION

Is Jesus' title as king threatening, disturbing, or troubling to you? Should it be? Take a few minutes to think seriously about it, and answer honestly.

In Luke 9:24–25 Jesus said, "If you try to hang on to your life, you will lose it. But if you give up your life for my sake, you will save it. And what do you benefit if you gain the whole world but are yourself lost or destroyed?"

Does Christmas remind you of this all-encompassing call to follow Jesus? In what ways do you, like Herod, unconsciously try to prevent Jesus from truly being king of your life?

This is not an easy teaching. If it is troubling to you or if you don't know what it means for Jesus to be king of your life, I encourage you to speak to a trusted Christian pastor, friend, or family member about it. *I also encourage you to talk to faithful believers about the overwhelming benefits of giving up your life for this Jesus.*

December 13

Matthew 2:9–11

King, Priest, Lamb

I'm a big fan of baby showers. In my opinion, all parents, particularly first-timers, ought to be showered with gear when their little tyke arrives. Everyone knows they will be sleep deprived and exhausted for the first six months, so the least we can do is pony up for a bundle of diapers or the latest helpful baby gadget.

When it comes to presents for newborns, the only thing worse than bringing no gift is bringing the wrong gift. I've seen this happen twice. When old friends christened their first child with a unisex family name (Casey), the handsome little boy received a bundle of pink clothes and girly goodies from one gift-giver who had failed to do any pre-birth research. In another instance, a disconnected family member gave a birthday card that boldly proclaimed, "It's fun to be forty!" Unfortunately for both the giver and the receiver, the birthday girl was only thirty-eight.

These are the kinds of gifts that result in awkward silence from other party-goers and an even more awkward "Thank you" as the guest of honor reacts to an embarrassing situation. It is the same kind of ungainly response I imagine Mary and Joseph gave when they accepted the third and final gift of the Magi.

51

The first gift given to Jesus was gold. No awkwardness there: everyone loves gold. It must have been an overwhelming moment as the poor carpenter and his young wife received the precious metal typically reserved for kings. Overtaxed by the Romans and underprepared for their first child, the gold would give them needed financial relief. The second gift, frankincense, was an aromatic perfume that had been used by priests for thousands of years, and while the gift may not have thrilled Joseph, Mary probably could not wait to unleash its beautiful aroma into their home. These two were welcome additions, but the third gift probably caught them off guard.

Myrrh was used at burials, both as incense and as an ingredient in ancient embalming fluid. It was not exactly a gift that screamed, "Congratulations! It's a boy!" The first two gifts brought honor, life, and beauty into the room, while the third brought thoughts of death.

At first blush no one would fault Mary and Joseph for offering the obligatory "Gee, thanks, you shouldn't have" before subtly tossing the myrrh out the window. But like every good story and every act of God, there was more to this gift than met the eye.

Gold was the substance of kings, frankincense a scent of priests, and myrrh an accoutrement of death. In all three God used the wise men's gifts to help Mary and Joseph back then, and you and me now, to understand the kind of man Jesus would become: our king, our priest, and the one who would die on our behalf.

52

REFLECTION

The next three devotions will focus on the powerful symbolism of the three gifts. For now spend a few minutes in silence, imagining that you were there at the manger watching as Mary and Joseph received their gifts. What do you feel?

Then turn the tables in your mind: if you had been the one bringing gifts to the baby Jesus, what would you have brought? Think creatively about a gift that you would have given that represents who Jesus is.

Spend a few minutes in prayer asking God to prepare your heart for what you will read in the next few days regarding these gifts. Ask him to give you wisdom and perspective on the kind of gift that Jesus is to the world.

December 14

Isaiah 9:6–7; John 1:1–4; Revelation 21:1-7

Gold: A Gift for a King

Kings come from kings, right? The son of a king takes the throne when his father dies. But what happens when the king is the King of kings—the eternal Father God who was never born and will never die? What happens when *that* king has a son? The answer lies in the mystery and the power of the Trinity.

Jesus was neither the human offspring of God (as were demigods in ancient Greek mythology), nor was he a regular human that was given divine status by God (as in Adoptionism, an early church heresy). Rather, Scripture reveals Jesus to be something unique: fully God and fully man. As fully God, he was the second member of the divine Trinity—made up of God the Father, God the Son, and God the Holy Spirit.

Look again at today's Scripture passages with this in mind. As you review them, think about the gold, shining with symbolism, that was presented to the newly born Jesus.

Seven hundred years before Jesus lived, Isaiah spoke one of God's brilliantly articulated prophecies about the King to come. Though a king, Jesus would not be like the Old Testament Israelite kings who wavered in their devotion to God, ruled according to their own selfish inclinations, and created far more war than peace. Instead, Jesus would act fully in accordance with God's will, care for his children selflessly, and usher in a kind of peace unknown to humanity: "He will be called: Wonderful Counselor, Mighty God, Everlasting Father, Prince of Peace" (Isaiah 9:6). Isaiah also prophesied that though he would be the Everlasting Father, he would be born into a very real time and place: "A child is born to us, a son is given to us" (9:6).

In a similar reversal, Isaiah proclaimed that though the Messiah would be born a child, his power would be complete and his rule would last forever: "The government will rest on his shoulders . . . and its peace will never end. He will rule with fairness and justice from the throne of his ancestor David for all eternity" (9:6–7).

The apostle John—after Jesus lived, died, rose again, and returned to heaven—also spoke about the eternal nature of Jesus the King. The baby that Mary had held in her arms was "the Word [that] gave life to everything that was created, and his life brought life to everyone" (John 1:4).

Jesus is also the one who will one day return to wrap up the story and carry us into our eternal future. John's revelation tells us that this child, who walked out of the grave, will one day permanently end all death, sorrow, crying, and pain (see Revelation 21:1–5).

The gold that the wise men brought for Jesus was far more than a generous gift from Mary and Joseph's baby registry. It was a symbol—a powerful symbol regarding the King of the universe, who lay in front of the Magi. Like a small nugget of gold that tangibly represents a vast wealth that existed long before the prospector found it, the swaddled child in the manger is the tangible reality of the God who existed long before and will remain long after the crowd who stood at his bedside. The gift of gold helps us remember that this child is that God: this child is that king.

REFLECTION

When you think of Jesus, do you think of him as the good King of creation who will return to rule again?

If so, take a few minutes to journal about what resonates with you in the expensive gift of gold brought to Jesus by the Magi.

If not, take a few minutes to journal about what holds you back from thinking of Jesus as king. Is it a lack of trust, a lack of faith, fear of letting go, misunderstanding about the role that the King should play in your life, or disbelief in the story altogether? Maybe it is something else. Honestly write out your thoughts.

If it is true that Jesus is the King who is the Wonderful Counselor, Mighty God, Everlasting Father, and Prince of Peace on whose shoulders the government will rest, is something resting on your shoulders that should be resting on his? What is it, and what is keeping you from releasing the desire and responsibility of being your own king and giving it to Jesus instead?

Read Matthew 11:28–30 slowly and repeatedly for five minutes, prayerfully letting the words wash over you.

December 15

Hebrews 4:14–5:9; 7:23–25

Frankincense: A Gift for the Priest

If you have attended church for a while, or if you have had any exposure to the Old Testament, you have likely either heard or read about the Old Testament priests. In the priests' days God restricted his presence to a special place within the tabernacle, and later the temple, called the holy of holies. The priests were a special group of Israelites, from the tribe of Levi, who had been chosen by God to step into his presence as representatives of the people. They were the only ones allowed to offer sacrifices for sin and communicate firsthand with the God of the universe. Often while in God's presence, the priests burned a sweet-smelling incense that filled the temple. What aroma was it? Frankincense.

This fact was not lost on the men from the Orient who visited Jesus. They brought frankincense, the incense of priests, because they believed that this baby would be the ultimate high priest who alone could stand before God on behalf of all people. As it turned out, they were right.

As today's reading puts it, Jesus "is able, once and forever, to save those who come to God through him. He lives forever to intercede with God on their behalf" (Hebrews 7:25).

Paul put it another way in Romans. He wrote that Jesus "is sitting in the place of honor at God's right hand, pleading for us" (8:34).

As if the reality of God the Son conversing with God the Father on our behalf is not wild enough, try this one on for size: Jesus prayed for *you and me* the night before his crucifixion. Wow! This is what he said:

> Father, I want these whom you have given me to be with me where I am. Then they can see all the glory you gave me because you loved me even before the world began! O righteous Father, the world doesn't know you, but I do; and these disciples know you sent me. I have revealed you to them, and I will continue to do so. Then your love for me will be in them, and I will be in them. (John 17:24–26)

This is why the Magi brought frankincense—because the baby they worshiped was Jesus, who had been with God the Father since before the world began. He was the Word made flesh, the Alpha and the Omega, the second member of the Trinity who has forever been and will forever be in conversation with the God of the universe on our behalf.

What the wise men believed of him is what the Bible teaches of him, and it is what you and I must know of him: Jesus the Christ is the one and only way for us to know God the Father (see John 14:6). Jesus is the priest who enters the holy of holies and opens the door to God on behalf of us all. We need no special education, unique bloodline, or particular rituals. We need only to confess our sin and turn our lives over to Jesus.

I wonder if Mary had any idea that night as she lit the frankincense and its sweet aroma filled her senses that the boy she was raising was the one high priest who would make a way to God for her and for everyone else. I wonder.

REFLECTION

Is Jesus someone whose birthday simply represents an opportunity for people to be with family and to open gifts? Or is Jesus the only one who can provide us the opportunity to be with God and to receive *his* gifts? Which is he for you?

Some of us think of our pastors or clergy as gatekeepers or as the special few who have direct access to God. How does Jesus' identity as the one and only high priest correct that mentality?

Take a moment to reflect honestly on these questions. Then consider praying this prayer:

God the Father,

I realize that I can step into your presence—right here and right now—only because of Jesus. Help me to recognize today what the wise men recognized about the newborn Messiah: that he is the only key that unlocks the door to God. Thank you for that, the most precious Christmas gift. Help me to open it often.

In the name of Jesus my high priest I pray, amen.

December 16

Romans 3:21–26; 8:1–3

Myrrh: A Gift for the Lamb of God

I'm not sure whether Mary and Joseph thought about the irony of the third gift while in the throes of new-parent delirium, but believers have been marveling at its meaning ever since it was given. The small box of myrrh sitting beside a young child presents a juxtaposition of opposites: birth and death, young and old, arrival and departure, hope and uncertainty, joy and sorrow.

Mary had been told that her son was God's chosen Messiah and that his "Kingdom [would] never end" (Luke 1:33). Yet Gentile strangers from the East had brought him a birthday gift that reeked of death. Ironically, it is in this seemingly ill-begotten funeral spice that the richest, most life-giving symbolism of all is found. This baby, like all the ones born before him, would die. But the death of *this* child would allow anyone who called upon his name to become a child of God. Through his death we all can experience real life.

We have learned about Jesus the King and Jesus the high priest, but today we will learn about Jesus the sacrifice. Kings and priests understood sacrifice. Every good king knew that the good of the whole was often contingent on the pain and suffering of a few. Every high priest knew that forgiveness required sacrifice to make atonement. But no king and no high priest had willingly offered his own life as the atoning sacrifice for the good of all. And none had been able. Yet in this innocent child Jesus, the world found a king and high priest who was both willing and able to be the Lamb slain so that others might live.

Do you remember John the Baptist's words when he first saw Jesus? He said, "Look! The Lamb of God who takes away the sin of the world!" (John 1:29)

Later Paul wrote, "When we were utterly helpless, Christ came at just the right time and died for us sinners" (Romans 5:6).

Jesus' words reveal his heart for us: "There is no greater love than to lay down one's life for one's friends" (John 15:13).

And a verse in Hebrews makes the powerful point that Jesus "offered himself as the sacrifice for the people's sins" (Hebrews 7:27).

You might think that interjecting verses about Jesus' death into the Advent setting darkens the Christmas narrative. But God did not choose a humble, unknown virgin girl to bear his Son because it would make a good story. Jesus did not give up his divine privilege (see Philippians 2:5–11) because he needed to know what it was like to be frail and helpless. The Son of God did not arrive in a backwater town of Jerusalem because he had a penchant for taking the scenic route.

Jesus was born to die. That *is* the Christmas narrative. He took on life as a man in order to give it away. He became like a human so that humans could become like him. His was not a grand experiment or an un-chaperoned prank; it was the very plan of God to offer you and me forgiveness, redemption, hope, and life abundant.

The wise men knew something that few others did: this baby was the King of kings, the one and only high priest, and the Lamb who would take away the sin of the world, and they celebrated his arrival while recognizing what he would ultimately accomplish for them and for us.

REFLECTION

Pray a prayer of thanks for God's sacrificial Son. You can write your prayer, say one out loud, or pray the one given here.

Jesus of Bethlehem, God of creation,

Thank you for coming to me. Thank you for leaving your divine privileges behind to fulfill the Father's plan of redeeming and saving his most beloved creation—people like me. Thank you, Jesus, for living a life that I cannot live and for dying a death that I could not have borne so that I might live with you now and in the life to come. Thank you, God, for not leaving us in our dying state but instead providing us a way out. Thank you for the great sacrifice you made on my behalf. Help me to live a life that honors you and introduces others to the abundant life available because of your sacrifice.

In the beautiful and strong name of Jesus I pray, amen.

December 17

Matthew 2:13–18

Hope in the Dark

As I write this, cable news outlets are ablaze with the story of Malaysia Airlines Flight MH17's mid-flight destruction over Ukraine. Unlike another Malaysian flight that disappeared over the South China Sea a few months earlier, this loss was no mystery. This plane and the lives of all 298 passengers and crew on it were purposely destroyed by Russian separatists involved in a violent takeover of Ukrainian land. The plane, a civilian airliner, was shot out of the air by evil people who wanted to destroy fellow human beings.

You might wonder what this has to do with today's scripture or how the retelling of such a dark incident serves any purpose in a book about Advent. But today's reading in Matthew 2:13–18 fills my heart with a deep and lasting sorrow, just as the heartbreaking news stories do today. Here, at the very beginning of Jesus' earthly life, is an account of great evil, deep suffering, and the kind of loss that would draw any person to questions about the goodness of God and the evil of humanity.

During this season of celebrating Christ's birth, we are often unaware of the deep pain and suffering of people around the world and down the street. Some of us look forward to Christmas and celebrate this season with an unbridled joy—the result of a wonderful year of good memories. Like Jesus and his family all those years ago, we and our loved ones have escaped the evil and darkness of the world around us and have much to celebrate.

However, many of us—perhaps you—feel as though there is nothing to celebrate. This year has not been one of health and triumph but of sickness and loss, pain and depression, sorrow and longing. Some of us have tasted of the realities of evil for the first time. We encountered bad people who seek our harm, opponents who seem impossible to love, and an enemy that has killed, stolen, and destroyed. Instead of celebrating, we mourn. Instead of looking forward in hope, we look forward in fear.

For others of us, even if the previous year has left us unscathed, darkness further back in our past tarnishes our souls or wrecks our emotions for yet another Christmas.

Like the mothers, fathers, brothers, and sisters of all the young boys murdered by Herod in Jesus' first year, we weep and mourn and wonder why.

Yet even in this kind of tragedy, hope is found. God is not bad because he allows such pain and suffering. God is good because he has sent his Son Jesus into the midst of our suffering to offer the one and only lasting solution. Jesus, who wept bitterly when his friend Lazarus died, who was enraged by the duplicity of the religious elite, who stared evil and death in the face and said, "It is finished," is acquainted with suffering and has come to fix it.

Jesus does not want you to deny the brokenness, loss, and evil of this world. He wants you to rely on him to solve it and to partner with him to relieve it. That was the hope that God gave everyone that first Christmas, and no matter the darkness around us, it is the hope that God gives us this Christmas.

REFLECTION

Make time to read the words of Jesus in John 16:33, the words about Jesus in Galatians 1:4, and the words about the future in Revelation 21:1–5. How do these verses provide you hope?

You probably know someone who is suffering through pain, sorrow, and loss this Christmas. Will you pray for that person now? Use the following prayer if it is helpful.

Dear God,

There is so much pain and suffering in the world, and some of it affects people I am close to. Will you be with _____ today? Will you meet my friends in their suffering and offer them relief? I ask that you will see justice and healing carried out where it is needed. Most importantly, I pray that you will help my friend to place eternal trust in you, knowing that one day all suffering will be finished, all pain will be gone, all tears will be dried, and all separation from you will end. I know that darkness and evil will not win the day. Thank you, Jesus, for understanding what it means to suffer and for offering us your comforting Spirit.

It is in the strong name of Jesus I pray, amen.

If you are the one suffering this Christmas, remember this: Jesus loves you, is present with you, and came to remedy *all* suffering. Pray the following prayer (or one of your own), and submit your true feelings to him.

Dear God,

I am suffering, and this time of year is particularly difficult for me. I want to join in the celebration of your Son's birth, but I struggle to see past the pain and sorrow I feel. Will you be close to me now? Will you keep my pain from swallowing me whole? Will you fight for what is right in this situation and heal that which is broken? I need you desperately. Thank you for promising to never leave me. I need you now. I trust that you will never leave me, and I lean on your presence, your friendship, and your power to help me move forward. While acknowledging that which is bad, I will still celebrate that which is good this Christmas. Thank you for Jesus.

It is in his all-powerful name I pray, amen.

December 18

Matthew 2:19–23

Loving and Sovereign, Free and Good

There is something remarkable about a God who grants freedom to us all yet remains in control of our circumstances. God allows the freedom for evil people to choose to destroy others' lives (like Herod and the terrorists we read about in yesterday's devotion), yet he maintains the power and control to assure that good will triumph (like Jesus' survival despite Herod's maniacal killing spree).

This kind of paradox can only be found in a God who is both loving and sovereign. If God does not allow freedom, then he is not loving. If he is powerless to affect the freedom he has given for the sake of good, then he is not sovereign.

I remember it like it was yesterday: I was crammed into a tiny car with three other would-be drivers and an instructor. It was the first day of driver's education, and I could almost taste the anxiety as four fifteen-year-olds got in the car. I have never been more thankful for growing up in a small Texas town where boys like me were driving tractors, boats, and our dad's pickup trucks well before puberty. I was comfortable behind the wheel. From the uneasy looks on the others' faces, however, it was clear that I was the only one who had received that kind of pre-driver's education training.

Once we were all seated and buckled, the first victim sat behind the wheel. The girl gripped the wheel so hard that the muscles in her forearms were about to explode. The poor thing would not take her eyes off the road, even though we weren't moving yet. Our instructor welcomed us and then pointed to the floorboard below his passenger side seat. None of us had ever seen a car with the brake pedal on the passenger side, and like all rookie drivers, we were terribly confused until our instructor graciously assured us that there was a brake pedal on the driver's side too.

He said, "I call this passenger side brake pedal my 'god pedal.' You have the freedom to drive, but I will always be able to control your speed so that everyone stays safe and we all arrive at our desired destination in one piece."

This is akin to God's love and sovereignty. In his love we are given the freedom to drive, to choose, to act, to stay on the road, or to veer off it. But in his sovereignty God maintains the power to accomplish, despite our actions, what he knows is best for all the passengers.

God had clearly told Joseph to protect the Son he had for many centuries been prophesying about. Egocentric narcissists with a God complex (Herod and his sons) had used their individual freedom to disobediently persecute the people, but God's sovereignty had ensured that the Messiah stayed safe. We needed Jesus then, and we need him now, so for our good (see Romans 8:28) the sovereign and loving God of the universe made sure that his Son survived those trying early years.

71

The same is true for you and me. Because of sin, we endure personal suffering and cause others to suffer in ways God never intended. But nothing will stop God's plan for the world's reconciliation in him. God is on a mission, and he will complete it. Matthew chapter 2 is proof positive.

REFLECTION

In what ways have trials and suffering led you to question God's love and sovereignty? In what ways have God's promises proven to be true despite your challenges of trials and suffering?

I recently asked a woman when she had most felt God's love. She answered, "When I was in chemo for cancer. I've never suffered more than I did then, and yet I've never felt God's love more." Do you think that is possible?

Do you think Joseph understood God's love though he and his family were running for their lives? Why or why not?

December 19

Luke 2:41–52

More than Family

Few stories of Jesus' life spark my imagination more than this one. When I read these eleven verses, I cannot help but wonder, what did Jesus look like when he was twelve? Was he mischievous without being sinful? Did he have boys and girls whom he called his friends? What were the rabbis thinking when they found themselves posing questions to a preteen instead of the other way around?

I recently watched a late-night talk show featuring a child prodigy. The fourth-grade boy played an electric guitar as if the spirit of Jimi Hendrix was inside him. It was fascinating. How had he become so good at such a young age? Most nine-year-old boys don't have the dexterity or mental focus needed to play a three-chord song, much less to perfectly recreate Chuck Berry's riffs in "Johnny B. Goode."

Jesus was not much older than that guitar-playing boy wonder when he was drawn into his heavenly Father's house to lead theological discussions with the rabbis. Later, on multiple occasions during his adulthood, Jesus made it clear that his role was to do only what God the Father was doing: "I tell you the truth, the Son can do nothing by himself. He does only what he sees the Father doing. Whatever the Father does, the Son also does" (John 5:19).

73

In Luke 2 we see that Jesus lived this out as a preteen. When his mother said, "Your father and I have been frantic, searching for you everywhere" (2:48), Jesus' response was as poignant as it was unexpected: "'But why did you need to search?' he asked. 'Didn't you know that I must be in my Father's house?'" (2:49).

Jesus' boyhood statement brings to my mind Luke 14, a passage we rarely spend time in because it describes a kind of discipleship to Jesus that we are not very comfortable with:

> A large crowd was following Jesus. He turned around and said to them, "If you want to be my disciple, you must hate everyone else by comparison—your father and mother, wife and children, brothers and sisters—yes, even your own life. Otherwise, you cannot be my disciple." (14:25–26)

The original Greek word for "cannot" is *dunamai*, which means "without ability, incapable." Jesus was not saying that those who do not give up their family and their own life to follow him are not *allowed* to be his disciple; he was (and is) saying they are not *strong* enough, *capable* enough, or *physically and morally powerful* enough to be his disciple.

Jesus Christ turns away no one who confesses him as Lord, repents of sin, and follows him. No one. But he is realistic about who is actually capable of the devotion required to be a true disciple.

If what we have read so far is true, and this child born in Bethlehem is also the Creator of the cosmos, the Redeemer of humankind, and the only real lover of our souls, then why would we not be more devoted to him than we are to our own families? Are our family members as devoted to us as Jesus is?

Jesus never teaches us to shun our family. But this story from his childhood gives us a glimpse of what it looks like to be more devoted to God than to any other.

REFLECTION

Do you struggle, as I do, with being more devoted to others (family, friends, colleagues) than to God? If so, write out one example of how you devote yourself to others instead of to God.

Now take a moment to write out why being devoted to God is worth more than being devoted to even those closest to you. If you do not believe that it is, write down the reasons why not.

Spend a few moments praying, asking God to show you the ways in which your devotion to others trumps your devotion to him, and ask him to give you the courage to take necessary steps to trust and follow him completely.

December 20

Read Hebrews 1:1–4

God Has Spoken

God is a storyteller, and the Bible is his book. His story began a long time ago when he spoke the world into existence and then created us, his crowning achievement in that glorious first chapter. Every word in Scripture that follows the creation is about God's relentless pursuit of our hearts, his redemption of humankind, and his eventual restoration of all creation. Over the last few weeks, we have been exploring the Advent portion of God's story—the scenes in which God introduces himself, in the flesh, as Jesus of Nazareth.

The Bible also contains commentaries on its unfolding narrative. These portions of Scripture are like study notes that help us grasp the truth and importance of God's story. In the past twenty days, we have rediscovered a portion of the story that God is writing, but today we turn our attention to a few passages that reveal to us why this story is so important.

I am grateful to God for my parents. Mom and Dad taught my siblings and me all we needed to know about life as Christ followers. However, I don't remember a word they said. What I remember is what they *did*.

I know right and wrong because my parents practiced it. I know how to read the Bible and pray because they did it. I know what commitment to a local church community looks like because they lived it. And I know how to create healthy relationships because I watched them do it. The words my parents spoke were also communicated by the way they lived.

God communicates with us in much the same way. The book of Hebrews begins with a profound statement: God "has spoken to us through his Son" (1:2).

Pause for a minute and chew on that. God (the eternal God of the universe) has spoken (communicated, revealed his character, explained himself) through his Son (Jesus the Messiah, the one who lay in a Bethlehem manger).

This is the narrative nature of God that we must get our heads around if we ever want to understand who God is. Who God is, what God wants, and how God will cure the world of sin are *not* explained by a set of propositions. They are not found in a list of rules—not even the Ten Commandments. They are found in Jesus Christ. When the author of Hebrews says that "God has spoken to us," he is talking about Jesus.

Jesus Christ is who God is, what God wants, and how God has solved the problem of sin, evil, and death.

In the person, work, and words of Jesus, we see what is best in the world, who created it, and what life is all about.

The apostle John recorded an important moment in which Jesus explained to Philip what it meant for him to be the Word of God:

> Have I been with you all this time, Philip, and yet you still don't know who I am? Anyone who has seen me has seen the Father! So why are you asking me to show him to you? Don't you believe that I am in the Father and the Father is in me? The words I speak are not my own, but my Father who lives in me does his work through me. (John 14:9–10)

John also recorded this: "Jesus explained, 'I tell you the truth, the Son can do nothing by himself. He does only what he sees the Father doing. Whatever the Father does, the Son also does" (John 5:19).

My parents aren't perfect, but what I saw them try to do is what Jesus did, and what Jesus did is what the Father did. And as the writer of Hebrews wrote, "The Son radiates God's own glory and expresses the very character of God" (Hebrews 1:3). Jesus is the very spoken word of God.

Want to hear God? Look at Jesus. Want to look at Jesus? Read the Scriptures and find a community that's trying hard to follow him. God will speak to you. And his words will always look like Jesus.

REFLECTION

What is a characteristic of God that you see most easily in Jesus? What is a characteristic of Jesus that you have seen in someone you know? How has God spoken to you through the life of Jesus and the lives of his followers?

Do you understand that you are part of God's story, not just someone who is supposed to obey a list of rules? If so, spend a few minutes writing down how your life fits into God's story. If you do not understand God's overarching narrative, commit to asking someone who does to help you find out where your life fits into God's grand story.

December 21

Romans 8:1–4

The Jesus Scan

Have you ever had a CT scan or an MRI? Computed tomography scans and magnetic resonance imaging machines are used by doctors to scan for medical problems in areas of the body where traditional x-rays are insufficient.

CT scans, like x-rays, are purely diagnostic. It would be fantastic if a doctor could say to someone with a brain tumor, "Just one more trip into the giant metal tube, and you'll be right as rain!" But that is not the purpose or capability of a CT scan. A scan can identify a problem, but it can do nothing to solve it. Scans reveal truth but offer no hope.

Because of our sinful nature, we have reduced God's good law into a type of CT scan. We often use the Old Testament law—in particular the Ten Commandments—solely as a diagnostic tool. We run our lives through its moral grid to see just how sinful we are. In some ways this is good. We are indeed a sinful people, and God's perfection brings that fact to light.

Paul acknowledges this in his letter to the Romans: "The law of Moses was unable to save us because of the weakness of our sinful nature" (8:3), he wrote. But this reality sets the stage for one of the most beautiful and gratitude-inducing verses in the entire Bible:

> So God did what the law could not do. He sent his own Son in a body like the bodies we sinners have. And in that body God declared an end to sin's control over us by giving his Son as a sacrifice for our sins. (Romans 8:3)

Jesus came on that first Christmas day to powerfully end sin's control over humanity. But we must be careful not to do to him what we are prone to do with God's law.

Do you remember WWJD bracelets? They were the wrist-bound trademark of Christians in the 1990s who believed that the essence of the Christian life was to ask, "What would Jesus do?" Presumably, if one could answer that question for any given situation and then act the way Jesus would have acted, one would have a firm grasp on the Christian life. I admire the gesture. But here's the rub: simply answering the question "What would Jesus do?" does not *empower* us to actually *do* it. Instead, it turns Jesus' life into a CT scan. When compared to our lives, the Jesus ideal only highlights the ways in which we must try harder, be more disciplined, and act better. And that's a problem.

A set of ideal rules, even if based on Jesus' life, is "unable to save us because of the weakness of our sinful nature" (8:3). We are not Jesus, and trying to be like him will not end sin's control over us. It will not save us. If anything, it will only frustrate and demoralize us.

What we need is a supernatural, all-powerful, paradigm-shifting event that can declare "an end to sin's control over us" (8:3). That supernatural, all-powerful, paradigm-shifting event is not a rule or creed or doctrine—it is the very person and work of Jesus the Christ. All we do is make room for his Spirit to move in us through confession, repentance, and baptism in the name of Jesus.

You see, the manger was not filled that Christmas morning with an ideal: it was filled with a bloody, crying, desperately helpless baby who eventually became the bloody, tortured, atoning sacrifice for our sin.

This is where many Christians struggle—but humankind is not saved by upholding an ideal. We are saved by a person. That person is Jesus, born on Christmas morning, and he stands for us when we cannot live up to our own ideals, much less his.

REFLECTION

If someone asked you to describe what it means to be a Christian, what would you say?

Read and think about Matthew 28:18–20. Why do you think Jesus told his followers to "make disciples" (28:19)

83

before teaching these new disciples to "obey all the commands" he had given?

If you are a Christian, is it because you successfully do the things Jesus did, or because you try to do so? Or are you a Christian because of something else? Take some time to reflect on your answers to these questions in light of the Scripture passages you read today.

December 22

Philippians 2:5–11

Though He Was God

Back in 2010 the TV show *Undercover Boss* began airing on CBS. Have you ever seen it? In each episode a CEO of some organization spends a week working at an entry-level position within his or her company. When the head honcho trades a business suit for the uniform and daily experience of a minimum-wage employee, it often moves the employee, the CEO, and the audience to tears. In the few episodes I have seen, employees have been deeply touched that the person at the top would venture to the bottom to work a day in their shoes.

The best moment in the show is the big "reveal," when the entry-level workers are told that the "rookie" next to them is actually their company's CEO. The reactions are priceless. Disbelief and gratitude mix with tears at the realization that the one running the show cares enough to enter the fray.

Though he was the CEO, he did not hold onto his lofty status.

Though she was the CEO, she humbly stepped into another's world.

The rich parallels between this scenario and today's passage are not difficult to see. The scripture begins with, "Though he was God . . ."

At Christmas we see clearly and poignantly the humility of our God. When we sing "Away in a Manger," "O Little Town of Bethlehem," and "What Child Is This?" we come closer to grasping Paul's words in Philippians 2. A baby is born in Bethlehem, but he is not simply a baby. This baby is the Son of God, the Creator of the universe, who "did not think of equality with God as something to cling to. Instead, he gave up his divine privileges; he took the humble position of a slave and was born as a human being" (2:6–7).

And like minimum-wage employees at a Fortune 500 company, we too are humbled and touched when our "CEO" steps into our shoes and lives as one of us.

In *Undercover Boss* the best CEOs take seriously the entry-level experience they gained and go on to use it to accomplish something meaningful for every employee. They have seen what is wrong in their company, and they step in to fix it so that every member of the organization can thrive. One might wonder if the creator of the hit show is a Christian, because today's scripture reveals that Jesus the Christ is the ultimate Undercover Boss.

Jesus is the Creator of the world (see John 1:3-4; Colossians 1:15–16), yet he experienced birth, childhood, the teenage years, and adulthood as a human being just as you and I have. He endured the same weakness, testing, and suffering as you and I have (see Hebrews 2:18; 4:15). Most importantly, he lived this life so that he could run a world in which every member could thrive (see John 10:10).

This capacity for us to thrive came not only through his life but by his death. In today's scripture we read, "When [Jesus] appeared in human form, he humbled himself in obedience to God and died a criminal's death on a cross" (Philippians 2:7–8). It was that death and the ensuing resurrection that defeated life's final enemy, paid for our sin, and modeled the ultimate kind of love. And because of it we can know God and have life that is truly life.

REFLECTION

In what areas of your life are you the "boss"? Have you ever thought about giving up your privileges for the sake of those you lead?

Consider the descriptions below and let God lead you into the service of others:

> Though you are the CEO, do you work for the benefit of your employees? Or do you cling only to the bottom line?

> Though you are a parent, do you stop to consider the perspective of your children? Or do you cling only to yours?

Though you are a teacher, do you seek to learn from your students? Or do you cling only to your own knowledge?

Though you are wealthy, do you give generously to those in need? Or do you cling to your security and privilege?

Though you are old, do you engage with the young and their new ideas? Or do you cling only to the way things used to be?

Though you are young, do you seek the wisdom of the old? Or do you cling only to your perspective and beliefs?

Though you are a pastor, do you allow yourself to humbly learn from your congregants? Or do you cling to your title?

What other types of authority or position do you cling to? How is God calling to you relinquish your "privileges" and take on the "humble position of a slave" for the benefit of others?

December 23

Colossians 1:15–20

What Child Is This?

One of my favorite Christmas songs is "What Child Is This?" It contains beautiful lyrics and a haunting score, and I cannot help but listen to it over and over again each Christmas season. It also contains the one question that was on everyone's mind that first Christmas morning.

Mary and Joseph, though told by an angel that this child was to be named "Jesus, for he will save his people from their sins" (Matthew 1:21), were no doubt asking, "What child is this?"

The shepherds heard from an angel in the midnight sky, "The Savior—yes, the Messiah, the Lord—has been born today in Bethlehem" (Luke 2:11), and in their joy-filled terror must have asked each other, "What child is this?"

The wise men "saw his star as it rose, and [they came] to worship him" (Matthew 2:2). In doing so evil King Herod and virtually everyone else in Jerusalem were caught in their wake, and they all wondered, "What child is this?"

A decade later the young Jesus was discovered "in the Temple, sitting among the religious teachers," who were "amazed at his understanding" (Luke 2:46–47). Even they must have posed the question, "What child is this?"

89

Christmas brings us back to the one question that every man and woman must eventually answer. Thankfully, the Bible provides that answer.

For today's devotion our Scripture passage will stand for itself. As you read this passage from Colossians, let the words wash over you, the identity of Christ amaze you, and the question "What child is this?" be forever answered for you.

> Christ is the visible image of the invisible God.
>
> He existed before anything was created and is supreme over all creation, for through him God created everything in the heavenly realms and on earth.
>
> He made the things we can see and the things we can't see—such as thrones, kingdoms, rulers, and authorities in the unseen world.
>
> Everything was created through him and for him.
>
> He existed before anything else, and he holds all creation together.
>
> Christ is also the head of the church, which is his body.
> He is the beginning, supreme over all who rise from the dead.
>
> So he is the first in everything.

For God in all his fullness was pleased to live in Christ, and through him God reconciled everything to himself.

He made peace with everything in heaven and on earth by means of Christ's blood on the cross. (Colossians 1:5–20)

REFLECTION

Read this passage three more times today (maybe at noon, at five, and one last time before you go to bed). Pay close attention to the attributes of Jesus that stand out to you, and listen carefully to God as you prayerfully consider them.

I rarely get past the last part of verse 16—"Everything was created through him and for him"—without stopping to ponder what that truly means. Which verse stops you? How does it shape the way you view the Christ child and who he was and is?

December 24

Ephesians 2:1–10

More than Just Christmas

Anticipation. Few words can better capture the feeling of Christmas Eve. For those of us who have children, Christmas Eve is bursting with impatient expectancy. Many of us can remember feeling as if we would explode if we had to wait even one second longer for Christmas to dawn. If some of us feel this way today, can you imagine what it was like on the first Christmas Eve?

How anxious the choirs of angels must have been as they prepared to sing the announcement into the Bethlehem sky.

How excited, nervous, and overwhelmingly eager Mary and Joseph must have felt as they waited to finally see their baby boy.

Imagine the enthusiastic and adventurous call the wise men felt as they studied the Scriptures for the sign of where the Messiah would be born.

Many of us restlessly sleep as we anticipate a gift, a good meal, a family gathering, or whatever brings us joy on Christmas day. But often our anticipation is short-lived. Our Christmas Eve anticipation is quickly spent on Christmas Day celebrations—and forgotten by the New Year's expectations. But if Christmas is only about the exciting rush of something new, then we miss the full picture.

Jesus was not a flash in the pan, no one-hit wonder, no fleeting moment. What we anticipate on Christmas Eve and celebrate on Christmas Day is much bigger than a single moment, a stunning announcement, or a solitary birth.

In his letter to the church in Ephesus, Paul describes it well. What we truly anticipate on Christmas Eve is Christ's *life*, not just his birth. Don't get me wrong—the fact that Almighty God descended to us is a powerful and valuable gift that cannot be overlooked. But it is not the *only* gift.

Jesus' incarnation made it possible for God to accomplish what he most wanted to accomplish: to raise us, his most beloved creation, from death in sin to new life in Christ.

Like the wise men's gifts, Paul's writing reminds us that Christmas is about our redemption: "Once you were dead because of your disobedience and your many sins," he wrote. "But God is so rich in mercy, and he loved us so much, that even though we were dead because of our sins, he gave us life when he raised Christ from the dead" (Ephesians 2:1, 4–5).

It would be shortsighted for a new parent to throw a delivery-room birthday party for his or her child but fail to look down the road at all the joys, trials, challenges, and victories that lie ahead for their newborn. So we too are shortsighted if we only anticipate Jesus' arrival and fail to celebrate the life that we know he lived.

The anticipation of Christmas Eve is not simply about the incarnation or the surprises of God or the gifts of one person to another. The anticipation of Christmas Eve is really about finally receiving the grace of God when we give our lives to his Son. Christmas is about the free gift of God that makes us right with him and grows in us the power to leave behind the selfishness that leads to death. Christmas is about the birth of Christ that preceded the death of Christ, both of which make it possible for us to live a life that matters.

REFLECTION

Take the time to read John chapters 13–17—the Upper Room discourse. How is Jesus' life about far more than Christmas?

Take time to journal or to write down a few sentences about how reading about Jesus' last days add value to celebrating his first.

December 25

John 1:1–18

Children of God

At various times throughout this Advent devotional, I have referenced verses from the first chapter of John. But today, on Christmas Day, I hope that you make time to slowly read this larger portion of the passage. As you do, let these eighteen verses about Jesus and the thoughts that follow in this devotion lead you to worship him.

John, one of the closest followers and friends of Jesus, wrote these immortal words from a deeply personal perspective. We can almost see the grateful, humble, and knowing smile on John's face as he penned them. He would have found it important, as the other Gospel writers would have, to trust the Holy Spirit's guidance as he sought to answer this crucial question: "What will the readers of this Gospel most need to know?"

This is one way he was led to answer that question: "To all who believed him and accepted him, he gave the right to become children of God" (John 1:12).

If I have written it once in this devotion, I have written it a thousand times: the message of Christmas is that Jesus—the child of God—has made it possible for you and me to become children of God. Yes, you. (Even you!) And me.

(Even me!) Children of the Most High, sons and daughters of the Almighty God! *This* is worth celebrating.

At our church we sometimes sing a modern hymn called "In Christ Alone." You may be familiar with it. A phrase in the third verse always moves me. Eight simple words stop me in my tracks: "For I am his, and he is mine."

Every time I sing it, a swell of disbelief and unspeakable gratitude rises from within me and moves me from the singing of words to the shedding of tears. I don't know why those words in that song impact me so deeply, but I think it is the same reason that verse 12 in John's first chapter chokes me up.

I am a child of God. He is my loving Father.

I am his, and he is mine.

On this Christmas Day, celebrate this with all your might. In Christ alone you are a child of the King. He came as a child so that you might become his child, and, unlike many of our earthly fathers, Jesus is the very definition of love. There is no selfishness in him, no misguided words, no broken relationship. He never leaves us and never forsakes us, and he takes great pride and delight in us. We are the apple of his eye, his crowning achievement, and he has left no obstacle standing that would keep us from his love.

The rest of the lyrics from "In Christ Alone" express it well. Read them with your mind, and be moved in your heart this Christmas Day.

> In Christ alone, who took on flesh,
> Fullness of God in helpless babe!
> This gift of love and righteousness,
> Scorned by the ones he came to save.
>
> Till on that cross as Jesus died,
> The wrath of God was satisfied;
> For every sin on him was laid—
> Here in the death of Christ I live.
>
> There in the ground his body lay,
> Light of the world by darkness slain;
> Then bursting forth in glorious day,
> Up from the grave he rose again!
>
> And as he stands in victory,
> Sin's curse has lost its grip on me;
> For I am his and he is mine—
> Bought with the precious blood of Christ.

Merry Christmas. Merry Christmas indeed.

REFLECTION

Christmas has come and with it the opportunity to become—or to be reminded that we are—children of God. What does being a child of God mean to you?

In what way does being a child of God impact the year you have ahead of you? And how might it impact the people around you?

If you truly lived as a child of the King in the year to come, what is one thing that you would consistently do? I encourage you to write it down, tell someone you know about it, and let your Father and your community help you follow it through.

The Next Twenty-Five Days

If you used this Bible study and devotional to prepare for celebrating Christmas, I hope that you do not stop here. Instead, I encourage you to commit to walking through the next twenty-five days in continued celebration of the coming of Jesus the Christ. Similar to the way you used the past four weeks as daily preparation for Jesus' birth, use the next four weeks to continue reading Scripture to engage with him personally. I hope that you will continue to read, pray, and share with others the hope that is found in knowing Jesus, the God of the universe who came to us on Christmas morning.

God is good, and in his Son Jesus Christ, there is much to celebrate and much to share with the world around us.

If you have any thoughts or personal reflections on what you have read, or if you would like to share how God moved, touched, or changed you during these twenty-five days, please send me an email. I would love to hear from you!

ChristopherGreerWriter@gmail.com.

About the Author

Christopher Greer is a writer, speaker, and church leader. He lives with his wife in Southern California. You can read more of his writing at www.Christopher-Greer.com and www.Trochia.org.

You can also find Christopher's Easter devotional, *Easter Is Coming,* at Amazon.com. *Easter Is Coming* is a thoughtful follow-up to *Christmas Is Coming* and will help you prepare for and celebrate Easter in a powerful way.

NOTES

NOTES

NOTES

Made in the USA
San Bernardino, CA
25 November 2016